CW00763372

a hurry of english

mary jean chan

**ignit**⚡**on**press

*For my parents,*
*who understand what poetry is for*

First published in 2018
by **ignition**press
Oxford Brookes Poetry Centre
Oxford Brookes University
OX3 0BP

Cover design: Flora Hands, Carline Creative
Page design: Thomas Nicolaou

A CIP record for this book is available from the British Library

ISBN 978-1-9997412-1-1

# Contents

*when we are silent*
*we are still afraid*

Audre Lorde

## Always

*Do you ever write about me?*
Mother, what do you think?
You are always where I begin.
Always the child who wanted to be
a boy, so you could be spared
by your mother-in-law.
Always the ear that hears you
translating my poems
with a bilingual dictionary.
Always the pen dreaming
it could redeem the years
you fled from, those
Red-Guarded days
and nightmares. Always
the mind's eye tracing
your frantic footsteps
towards the grandfather
I would never meet.
Always the lips wishing
they could kiss those mouths
you would approve of.

# what my mother (a poet) might say

~~that she had scurvy as a child~~
~~that I don't understand hunger until I can describe what a drop~~
~~of oil tastes like~~

*that Mao wrote beautiful Chinese calligraphy*

~~that she finds democracy to be the opiate of the masses~~
~~that I am a descendant of the Yellow Emperor~~

*that Mao wrote beautiful Chinese calligraphy*

~~that she dreams about seeing her father's heart in the doctor's fist~~
~~that I must only write about flowers~~

*that Mao wrote beautiful Chinese calligraphy*

~~that she showed her mother-in-law a blood-speckled sheet~~
~~the morning after~~
~~that I shall love a man despite his strength~~

*that Mao wrote beautiful Chinese calligraphy*

~~that she wants to devour me back into herself~~
~~that I would be *ci sin* to love another woman~~

*that Mao wrote beautiful Chinese calligraphy*

~~that her neurons are a crumbling Great Wall~~
~~that I am a new earth arising from hierarchies of bone~~

*that Mao wrote beautiful Chinese calligraphy*

# How It Must Be Said

What isn't obvious isn't obvious because I intend to obfuscate. O chews its own tail like a rabid dog. What does it say about me, this obsession written in a language I never chose? My desires dressed themselves in a hurry of English to avoid my mother's gaze. How I typed "Shakespeare", then "homoeroticism + Shakespeare" into Google, over and over. My mother did not understand the difference between English words, so she let me be. A public history seeps into the body, the way tea leaves soak up the scent of a fridge. An odourless room is not necessarily without trauma. We must interrogate the walls. My skin is yellow because it must. Love is kind because it must. Admit it, aloud.

# There is No Memorial for This in China

My mother tries to mourn a war
whose face is her own. His face
still hangs in the sacred square.
She whispers *He is a demigod,*
*don't you dare.* I tell her he is
not worth the spit on my tongue –
in any language. *Try anger for once,*
*won't you?* I visit one of his homes
in Qingdao, admire the bourgeois
upholstery. I scan the floors to find
something to take back to my mother
as proof he is human: a nail clipping
perhaps, so she can place it beneath
her heel and crush it. Instead, I say
the food was delicious, the weather
held. I fail to mention my heresies.

## Practice

As a teenager, fencing was the closest thing
I knew to desire, all the girls swapping one

> uniform for another before practice, their white
> dresses replaced by breeches. I thought we were

princes in a fairy tale with a twist, since
there were no princesses to be taken, wed.

> As knights, we were told to aim for an imaginary
> spot just above our opponent's left breast. Often,

I left a bruise: the blade's tip ricocheting off chest-
guards onto flesh. Just as often, I would feel yellow

> blooms of ache where the girl I thought was beautiful
> had pierced my heart. Hours later, I would transform.

I would head back home with a deepening
sense of dread, my bruises fading to quiet.

# Dress

The same uniform for twelve years. A white skirt, blue collar, blue belt, blue hem. A dark, no-nonsense kind of blue. White like snowfall in Eden. You washed it every single day, made sure you ate in small bites, always wore an extra pad so none of the blood could seep through. You began wearing that dress at the age of six, your skin haunted by the British flag, so you could be *Chinese with English characteristics*. Each time you wore that uniform, you shut your body up. Some girls wore theirs short, discoloured, tight. As Head Girl, you reported them to the Headmistress's office for inappropriate behaviour, kept your own dress clean, at just the right length.

Most mornings, you see the face of a boy in the mirror. You expect to fall in love with him, someday. Meanwhile, your fingers brush the wrist of another girl as you jostle into the assembly hall, and you understand that sin was never meant to be easy, only sweet. What memory might light up the pond you sat beside in dreams, eyeing so much depth it would be years before you dared? What curvature of tongue might you taste, as if another's breath were blessing? One night, you find yourself back there, kneeling beside the pond. You dream. A voice whispers *Hell is not other people*. You slip into the water, stripped of the glowing dress you wore for thousands of days.

# At the Castro

*for Orlando*

the first time you stepped
was the first time
not just a shuffle
but limbs loosening
toes into tambourines
whispering
the press of thigh
strange hands that
they start to steer
of your body
waters
flooding the room
the girl who thought she had to
for the rest of her life
became the wind
till you became sober
ashamed
smiled
another girl
of mouths
become holy
our own sighs
four years later
the music stops
were shot before
what if you had been
the bullet
would you have
would you have known
clutch
the way skin
but always

into a gay bar
you danced
or nodding to music
into whiplash
your tongue
*oh my god*
against wall
love you so much
the shipwreck
into open
liquid light
that night
sit down
broke all the rules
you drank
enough not to be
the boy you never were
kissed
a cathedral
this is how heretics
by setting
on fire
a hand pulls a trigger
how many
their first kiss
stopped by
into whose arms
surrendered
the anguished
of your lover's breath
is never an apology
an act of faith

7

## Conversation with Fantasy Mother

Dear fantasy mother, thank you
for taking my coming out
as calmly as a pond accepts a stone
flung suddenly into its depths.

You sieved my tears, added
an egg, and baked a beautiful cake.
You said *Let us celebrate, for today*
*you are reborn as my beloved.*

The candles gleamed and the icing
was the colour of truth — creamy white —
coated with the sweetness of
sprinkles. We sat together

at the table and ate. Afterwards,
I returned to my room and touched all
the forbidden parts of myself, felt
a kindness I had not known in years.

## They Would Have All That

To sing the evening home, she prepares a pot
of lentil stew, her phone radiant with messages,
imagining her lover's steady hand gripping her
smartphone to navigate towards some notion

of home, their flat now a familiar place of worship,
their bodies growing close and moving apart
with the regularity of heartbeat, hot breath.
There the lover is, running to catch a bus,

wondering at her lover's motions throughout
the flat, how her feet must press on the floor
with each step, how the orchid must have
stretched itself a few millimetres overnight,

how the stew must be whispering on the stove
and the table laid for dinner. They are gentler now
because they have memorised each other's fears
like daily prayer: how too much salt brings back

the years of loneliness, how a bath may be more
necessary than a rough kiss after a day's drought
of tenderness. They are gentler because they have
grown too knowledgeable to love any other way.

*Have I hurt you?* Such asking becomes routine,
almost like walking down the aisle of a supermarket
at evening, but it is what they do best. Beyond desire:
two clasped bodies holding the heart's ache at bay.

//

My mother lays the table with chopsticks and ceramic
spoons, expects you to fail at dinner. To the Chinese,

you and I are chopsticks: lovers with the same anatomies.
My mother tells you that *chopsticks* in Cantonese sounds

like *the swift arrival of sons*. My mother-tongue rejoices
in its dumbness before you as expletives detonate: *[two*

*women] [two men] [disgrace]*. Tonight, I forget that I am
bilingual. I lose my voice in your mouth, kiss till blood

comes so *sorry* does not slip on an avalanche of syllables
into sorrow. I tell you that as long as we hold each other,

no apology will be enough. Tonight, I am dreaming again
of tomorrow: another chance to eat at the feast of the living

with chopsticks balanced across the bridges of our hands
as we imbibe each *yes*, spit out every *no* among scraps of

shell or bone. Father says *Kids these days are not as tough*
*as we used to be. So many suicides in one week.* How many

times have you and I wondered about leaving our bodies
behind, the way many of us have already left? My friend's

sister loved a woman for ten years, and each word she says
to her mother stings like a papercut. Each word she does

not say burns like the lines she etches carefully into skin.
I have stopped believing that secrets are a beautiful way

to die. You came home with me for three hundred days —
to show my family that dinner together won't kill us all.

# Rise and Shine

This morning your voice is a cleft wing and the sky
is all echo. The therapist says *Avoid the foetal position*
*because there will be too much blood*
*concentrated around the vital organs* —

by which she means *Try to sit up*
*and greet the day anew.* When air becomes a cage.
When breathing demands concentration:
a striving of muscle and sinew.

When syllables transmute into blabber, hiccup,
torrent leaking from every orifice on your devastated face.
Your voice is a river running deep underground.
Your lover asks for language, and you cannot give it.

Last night the faucet broke, and you cursed the water
for failing you. You have had enough
of water — that embryonic fluid that broke you
onto this patch of earth, screaming

and alone. Water reminds you of your mother's
grief, so you down three glasses and wish the icecaps
across the Arctic would flood the world into oblivion.
Your lover's voice is so utterly ordinary

in its pain that you could almost empathise.
*How did we survive?* You whisper this
into her breasts, her hands smoothing your brow,
her voice in your ears like weather.

# Notes Towards an Understanding

I

When you said *Why didn't you warn me
about cultural differences?* I didn't know
whether you meant my mother's face all
darkened like a curtain, or the vegetables.

II

When mother said *The contours of her ears
are calamitous*, I momentarily reflected on
my own auditory shells – whether they too
played a part in my irrevocable queerness.

III

When father said *I find language to be a
very difficult thing*, I wondered if he was
apologising for his silences, how he said
nothing when mother detonated my name.

IV

When I said *I want to shout at all of you, but
in which language?* My mind was tuned to
two frequencies: mother's Cantonese rage,
your soothing English, asking me to choose.

## Dragon Hill Spa

*Seoul, South Korea*

It is the year 2016, but you know
how women tame their own bodies

into bones, dig their own graves in
daylight. Here, for once, in a hot bath

of rainbows, the bodies let themselves
go, the water holds them up to the light,

the lips murmur a prayer to skin. Here,
the only hands that touch their wrists

are their own. Here is no-man's land.
Here, the names of soldiers, heavy-

handed, are forgotten. Here, no one
takes what they want from the women

whose gods are freely chosen,
whose bones are theirs to bury.

# Wet Nurse (Shanghai, 1953)

*for the woman who raised my mother*

The milk pours from my body into
a strange mouth. It is always hungry
and so am I. The *Yulan* magnolias
are rioting in the garden, unruly
children bored with yet another spring.
The mouth frees my nipple and leaks
tributaries down my skin. It has been
ninety-seven days since the city stole
my flesh. My husband and I have not
spoken since. He shall never touch me
again. When the mother goes to preach
the gospel, I pretend I am her, holding

my own daughter, promising to never
let go. The baby sees no problem with
two mothers. The father adores her from
a distance. Sixth child, third daughter,
beloved one. Some nights, I moan as if
to say *forgive me*. I long for a landslide
in the mind, so I might bury the moment
when I abandoned my daughter on a train
the morning of her birth, weak from blood-
loss and fearful that *a wet nurse with child will
never find work*. Now, a baby smiles up at me,
another brushes my breast with phantom lips.

# When I Say That My Mother Cooked

I mean that *manang* did, her overworked fingers
dipping into the wok for a quick baptism of fire, testing
the sauce for sweetness, knowing that sheer perfection
would stave off my mother's wrath, earn her a compliment
and perhaps a hundred Hong Kong dollars to add to her wages.

I called her *dear* in Ilocano, a Filipino language
she taught me in brief interludes as I grappled with my heritage:
pre-colonial Cantonese and post-colonial English. Her songs
would be for playtime, when she would sing to me
as I was getting ready for sleep:

*Manang Biday, ilukatmo man
'Ta bintana ikalumbabam
Ta kitaem 'toy kinayawan
Ay, matayakon no dinak kaasian*

*Dear Biday, please open
Open your window
So you can see the one who adores you
Oh, I will die if you do not care*

My mother fired her for some reason I never understood,
though I pleaded for *manang* to stay, and for *manang* who came
after to never leave me again. They learnt to cook my mother's
hometown into life – raising Shanghai through steam –
dishes so pungent you could not tell whether

my mother had left the kitchen at all, *manang* so adept
at curating flavours she made our Chinese guests praise
all the chefs in the house, my mother sometimes gracious,
hollering *manang's* name so they might acknowledge
her talent and labour, only for her to return

to the kitchen for more cleaning,
after all the guests had left, after
I had climbed into bed; *Manang Biday*, a tune
I still hum whenever I remember her, my *manang*,
who taught me how to sing.

## Rules for a Chinese Child Buying
## Stationery in a London Bookshop

Speak to the white
elderly man at the counter.
There will be many

more of them
in your life, but start
with him. Recall those syllables

you've whispered over and
over like some version
of the Lord's Prayer:

*Our Father who art*
*in heaven and is*
*white and beyond skin.*

Enunciate. He must hear
what you have to say
if you are to be helped.

Begin with *please*. Say
*may I*. End with *thank you*.
He will be delighted

to know you are polite,
soft-spoken, well-mannered.
You will be overjoyed

at his acceptance, a palm
reaching towards you
for something you are able to give.

You must hand over the money
quickly, but not in haste.
Your parents' wisdom comes

from *having had more salt*
*than you have eaten rice.*
This proverb is untranslatable,

but memorise and trust
in it all the same.
You are a tiny machine

being oiled
for the day you must face
the world, a lifetime

of swallow and spit
ahead of you, years of salt
and rice and tea.

## The Horse and the Monkey

I tell you that I am a horse, you
a monkey, fated by the Chinese
zodiac *to remain together as long*
*as both partners practise the art*
*of compromise.* Three hundred
and sixty-five days. The horse
and monkey can now be found
riding the wind at the fifth base
of Mount Fuji. We hold each other
as if our limbs were the mountain's
melting snow. All those days when
I believed the odds were bruised –
our zodiacs, my Chinese parents.
Your tofu skin against the butter
of mine. Moments before the plane
delivers us to ground, I beg amidst
the turbulence – *Please* – to Buddha,
even to the Lord who would never
grant me permission to love you.
I am bargaining with these whorls
of steel to keep going, in spite of
everything. At home, my mother
greets us both with the words *I love*
*monkeys. They are very auspicious*
*creatures.* In that moment, did you
realise that we were being blessed?

## Love for the Living

What does it mean to want to live?
Only this: to refuse to see the mouth's anguish
as a sign to step out of an open window.
To refuse to be twenty-six and afraid of leaving
one city for another. To refuse to be a bomb
shelter for your mother's fears. What is it like
to believe the night isn't a cemetery
for bodies like yours? Like this: the joy at a spiral
of rainbow bunting scattered like relief
across a lit sky. The ache of pleasure when
your mother mentions your lover's name.
The way you notice – over and over, with incredulity –
when no one seems to care how you stand
in the open, kissing and holding hands.

# Long Distance

You are running on the rain-dark pavement through Sutton Park. Where I am, sun. All the dehumidifiers are on in the house. No fireplaces. Some seas are colder than others, some bodies warmer. I am drinking Iron-Buddha: tea leaves waiting for their time to blossom. It is too spring here for my own good, too much green in the salad bowl. Too many stories of salvation; earlier, blue beyond belief. The moon is lying on its back in my dreams. What a smile looks like. A toothbrush touches my lips. Asian steamed sea bass for dinner, with white rice. Polar bears have black skin. Victoria Harbour was named after your Queen. How many hearts in a deck of cards shuffled across two continents? I am catching a plane tonight, thinking about the map on your neck.

## The Translator

The year sinks into its own bath, blinking
slowly into breath. *Your face looks like a lit
Confucian lantern* my mother observes –
as I translate her questions for my lover
whose Chinese is a riddle well-told.
Tonight, I empty olive oil into my ears,
bless both feet with crushed ginger and
honey to ring in the first year when
my mother jokes that I am no longer
her mistake. A translator: *one who is fully
bilingual, refusing soil and other forms of burial.*

## Tea Ceremony

There are days when I pretend
to understand my mother's grief,

as I coax her into sitting at the table
for a tea ceremony, so she might linger

on the rush of green into glass,
how the scent of leaf dissolves

both past and future in one gulp.
We drink in a serene silence,

my mother smiles a smile that
breaks my breath into laughter.

She is radiant now, lost in the kettle's
repetitive chant, her gaze fixed on

the dance of fingers between utensils.
I love my mother's joy, her reprieve

from the sorrow of Red-Guarded nights.
Time is a wound she adorns with designer

clothing and too many sleeping pills.
I tell her *Go to bed*. She says *I can't*.

*Can you stay?* As a child, I dreaded
her desperate need, my hand resting

on her forehead, unable to let go.
Even now, with Freud and Jung

as bedside reading, I can only
invite her to the table: *Look,*

*mother, your hands are beautiful.*
*Look, mother, our tea is ready.*

# Acknowledgements

Grateful acknowledgements are made to the editors and publishers of the following publications in which some of these poems first appeared: *Ambit, Bare Fiction Magazine, English: Journal of the English Association, The London Magazine, Magma, PN Review, The Poetry Review, The Rialto* and *The Scores*.

Epigraph is taken from Audre Lorde, 'A Litany for Survival', in *The Black Unicorn* (W.W. Norton & Company, Inc., 1978).

My heartfelt thanks to Briony Bax for nominating '//' for the 2017 Forward Prize for Best Single Poem (Shortlisted), to Daljit Nagra for selecting 'Wet Nurse' as the winner of the 2016 Oxford Brookes International Poetry Competition (ESL), and to Helen Mort for awarding 'At the Castro' Third Place in the 2016 Bare Fiction Prize for Poetry.

Special thanks to Professor Jo Shapcott for her ongoing mentorship and support, and to Royal Holloway, University of London, for the 2014/15 International Excellence Scholarship and the 2015 University of London MA Creative Writing Prize that enabled me to write these poems.

FSC
MIX
Paper
FSC® C004754